I0164459

The InterWar Years

(1919~1939)

THE BEST ONE-HOUR HISTORY

Robert Freeman

The Best One-Hour History™
Kendall Lane Publishers, Palo Alto, CA
Copyright © 2014, Robert Freeman
All rights reserved.
ISBN-978-0-9914096-0-0

Contents

The Path From World War I to World War II

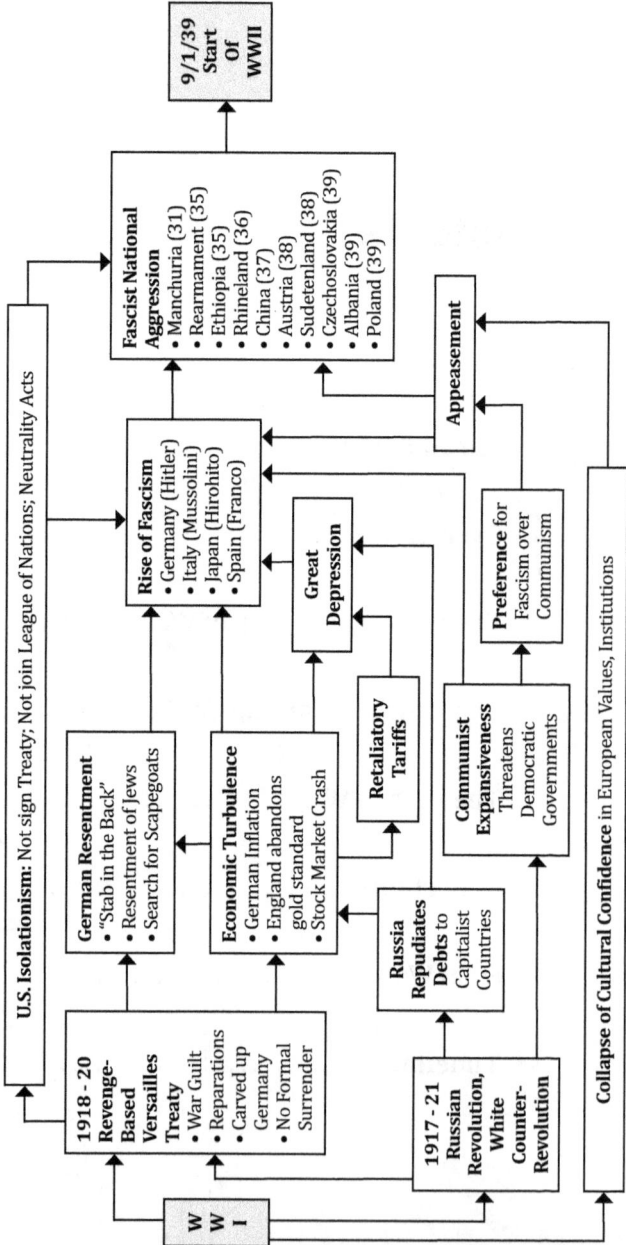

1910's **1920's** **1930's**

U.S. Isolationism: Not sign Treaty; Not join League of Nations; Neutrality Acts

Fascist National Aggression
- Manchuria (31)
- Rearmament (35)
- Ethiopia (35)
- Rhineland (36)
- China (37)
- Austria (38)
- Sudetenland (38)
- Czechoslovakia (39)
- Albania (39)
- Poland (39)

9/1/39 Start Of WWII

Rise of Fascism
- Germany (Hitler)
- Italy (Mussolini)
- Japan (Hirohito)
- Spain (Franco)

Appeasement

German Resentment
- "Stab in the Back"
- Resentment of Jews
- Search for Scapegoats

Economic Turbulence
- German Inflation
- England abandons gold standard
- Stock Market Crash

Great Depression

Preference for Fascism over Communism

Retaliatory Tariffs

Communist Expansiveness
Threatens Democratic Governments

1918 - 20 Revenge-Based Versailles Treaty
- War Guilt
- Reparations
- Carved up Germany
- No Formal Surrender

Russia Repudiates Debts to Capitalist Countries

1917 - 21 Russian Revolution, White Counter-Revolution

Collapse of Cultural Confidence in European Values, Institutions

WWI

1 Introduction

At the eleventh hour of the eleventh day of the eleventh month of 1918, all was quiet on the Western Front. The most bloody war in the history of the world was over. But within only another twenty years, Europe would be back at war, with a new generation of fresh young men ready to be thrown to the slaughter. And this next World War, the Second, would prove even more devastating than the First. More than 50 million people would die, versus only 10 million in the First. Economic damage would be ten times what it was in the earlier war. Genocide would become a formal act of national policy.

What happened in these twenty brief years that led from one World War to the next? Why did the calamity of the First World War not provide reasonable men the means to avoid the Second? In fact, why did the events and settlement of the First World War seem to make the Second World War all but inevitable? And was it, in fact, inevitable, or, was it a matter of choice?

This book addresses the years 1919 to 1939: The World Between the Wars. It explores the poisoned legacy of World War I and how that legacy laid a path directly to World War II. It explains the major events that happened in this period and how each added fuel to what would become the fire of war. It details the sequence of events that led to the lighting of the fire and the start of World War II. Finally, it briefly examines why Hitler was so successful in seducing Germany to its doom and why the Western democracies were so unsuccessful in resisting Hitler's aggression.

If ever there were a society that had lost its moorings, even its sanity, it was Europe in these InterWar years. The "Great War," as the First had been called, had destroyed not only vast empires and centuries of accumulated wealth, it destroyed Europeans' own belief in their judgment, their values, their institutions, and their competence to produce a shared, durable peace. They tried to navigate these years with a kind of ad hoc-ery, imagining that the world that had been still was. But it wasn't. Because of their inability to recognize this, Europeans surrendered control of their civilization to a mad man who plunged it into the greatest horror the world has ever known. This is that story.

2 Overview

The First World War had inflicted great trauma on Europe. Beyond the unimaginable destruction itself was the sickening recognition that nobody had been able to stop it. Then, the 1919 Treaty of Versailles that settled the War was a treaty of vengeance, intended by the French to bleed the Germans white so they could never again attack France. It stripped Germany of all of its colonies, created new nations on its periphery that contained millions of German people, and imposed reparations that made it extremely difficult for the German economy to recover from the devastation of the War.

A new government was installed in Germany, the Weimar Republic. But the German people knew nothing of republican government. They had lived for centuries under an authoritarian monarchy. Worse, the right wing oligarchs, industrialists, and militarists who had started, overseen, and lost the First World War were not about to give up power. They conspired from the beginning to undermine the Weimar government.

They would eventually succeed, placing Adolph Hitler at the head of government. But not yet.

Almost immediately following the "peace," Germany fell behind in its payment of reparations to France. France responded by occupying an important coal producing region of Germany, the Ruhr. The German government told its workers to carry out passive resistance—to pretend to work, but not. But it had to pay their wages, and so began printing money. This set off one of the greatest inflationary spirals in history, destroying the German currency and wiping out the German middle class. Out of the ashes of this financial catastrophe arose Adolph Hitler, stoking the flames of resentment of the Treaty of Versailles and the nations which had imposed it.

The larger problem was that England and France owed money to the U.S. for repayment of the loans that the U.S. had made to them to finance the War. To earn those funds, they needed the reparations payments from Germany. This problem was solved by the 1924 Dawes Plan where the U.S. agreed to loan money to Germany, which would use it for its reparation payments to England and France, who would then use those funds to make their payments to the U.S. This convoluted scheme worked well enough as long as the U.S. continued loaning money to Germany.

But in 1929, the U.S Federal Reserve Bank, trying to cool an overheating stock market, began raising interest rates. This had the effect of drawing money back to the U.S., making it impossible for the Europeans to make their chains of payments. The higher rates also set off a collapse in the stock market, vast destruction of paper wealth, and the resultant Great Depression. Industrial production plummeted, commodity prices collapsed, and incomes fell throughout the world. Germany was hit especially hard. It had suffered the Great Inflation only six years earlier and its economy was precariously dependent on loans from the U.S. By 1932, German unemployment had hit an all-time high of 45%. For the third time in just over a decade the German people suffered calamitous economic devastation.

This collapse played into the hands of the German communist party, which drew millions of recruits from the ranks of the unemployed. To forestall communist gains, German President Paul von Hindenburg appointed Adolph Hitler, head of the German National Socialists Workers (Nazi) Party, to the post of Chancellor. Hitler promised Hindenburg and the right-wing industrialists he represented that he would ban labor unions and crush communist opposition. He kept his promises. Within months, he banned competing political parties, suspended civil liberties, and implemented one-party rule.

Hitler's ideology, Nazi-ism, was a derivative of what Benito Mussolini had implemented in Italy in the 1920s: fascism. It was a patchwork of corporate/state capitalism, nationalist aggression, and single party rule, all carried out through pervasive propaganda and intense social regimentation. It was popular with the German people for a variety of reasons: Hitler gave people an excuse to blame others for their problems; he told them that they were superior to the people of other nations and races; and he implemented an aggressive program of military rebuilding that almost completely eradicated unemployment.

Upon gaining power, Hitler began repudiating the Treaty of Versailles. He rearmed the military beyond the limitations permitted by Versailles, and occupied the Rhineland which separated France and Germany. This, too, was forbidden by the Treaty. Curiously, the Western democracies, led by England and France, did not challenge Hitler. Indeed, England not only excused these actions and rationalized them in public, it informed France that it would not back France if it stood up to Hitler. This effectively destroyed the collective security regime that lay at the heart of the settlement of World War I. The result was that it became harder and harder to stand up to Hitler's subsequent aggressions.

Hitler capitalized on this capitulation by accelerating his campaign of nationalist aggression. In the spring of 1938, he annexed Austria, again against the prohibition of Versailles but with the public support of the leader of England, who declared that he "understand(s) the German desire for national unification."

In the fall of 1938 Hitler demanded that Czechoslovakia cede to Germany part of its territory called the Sudetenland. The Sudetenland contained some three million Germans and vast mineral and industrial resources. At a meeting in Munich in September 1938, the leaders of England, France, and Italy decided to hand the Sudetenland over to Hitler. Czechoslovakia was not represented at the meeting. This was the high point of "appeasement" of Hitler by the Western powers

In the spring of 1939, Hitler seized the rest of Czechoslovakia, despite his promise at Munich that he would not. As with all of Hitler's prior aggressions, the Western democracies did nothing. In August 1939, Hitler signed a non-aggression pact with Russia assuring that neither country would attack the other should either of them attack Poland, which lay between them. This amounted to an implicit agreement to divide Poland between them. It also gave Hitler the assurance that he could fight a one-front war. (It was the fact of a two-front war that had doomed Germany's efforts in World War I and German generals were adamant that such a situation must be avoided again.) Hitler attacked Poland on September 1, 1939, thus beginning World War II.

Several themes echo through this twenty year period. The first is the damaging consequence of Versailles. It would become the very model of how *not* to settle a major international problem. Another theme is the long shadow cast by the imposition of communism in Russia during World War I. The Russians suspected that England fostered Hitler's growth in the expectation that he would attack and destroy Russia, much as the German armies had done during World War I. British Prime Minister Neville Chamberlain, notorious for the appeasement at Munich, apparently never imagined Hitler would instead use his new strength to attack the West.

Another theme that pervades the period is economic turbulence, from the Great Inflation of the Twenties, to the Great Depression of the Thirties. This unquestionably created a fertile field in which Nazi extremism took root. A final theme is the collapse of Western will in standing up the most odious, indeed destructive, impulses of German, Italian, and Japanese militarism. It was this failure of political will—or perhaps we should call it the preference for capitalist dictatorship over communist dictatorship and the inability to understand its consequences— that made all but inevitable a Second World War in less than a generation.

3 The Poisoned Legacy of World War I

World War I cast a looming shadow over the decades that followed it. In three important ways, World War I conditioned and channeled the responses of Europeans as they tried to recover from it. Those were: the specter of communism; the fundamental flaws of the Treaty of Versailles; and the withdrawal of the U.S. from engagement in the world community. The combination of these forces allowed, even promoted, the very worst impulses in European politics.

The Specter of Communism

Even before World War I was over, the specter of communism began to haunt the Western democracies. Russian society was fragile. It was industrially backward, in fact virtually feudal, and desperately poor. So, when order broke down following the German invasion of Russia in World War I, the Russian Czar was overthrown. In 1917, a small cabal of communist revolutionaries led by Vladimir Lenin carried off the Russian Revolution, one of the most momentous events of the twentieth century.

The new government immediately declared its intent to spread communist revolution throughout the world. This posed a direct threat to democratic capitalist governments. Western governments responded by invading Russia to try to overthrow the new government. This "White Counter Revolution" of 1920 - 1921, led by the United States, Britain, and France, failed but set an adversarial tone that would poison relations between Russia and the West for the rest of the century.

The communist threat to capitalist governments became especially acute in the 1930s, when capitalist economies collapsed in the Great Depression. Tens of millions of workers were unemployed in the West, but the Russian economy boomed. Between 1928 and 1938, British manufacturing grew by 17%. Russian manufacturing, however, exploded, growing more than 400%. Workers in capitalist countries began to favor communism and to join communist political parties. In 1932, 80% of the German communist party was made up of unemployed people. Capitalist governments tried to isolate Russia, keeping it out of European affairs. They also tolerated and even encouraged Japan's predations in Asia because they posed a counterweight to Russia's influence in Europe.

The West's hatred of communism was so deep that by the mid-1930s, when democratic governments faced two mortal enemies—communism and fascism—they chose fascism as the lesser of two evils. France, and especially England, adopted policies that tolerated fascism over communism and that in some cases encouraged it. Repeatedly, Western Europe's democracies rebuffed Russia as it offered help against the rising power of German militarism. When, on the brink of war in 1939, Russia virtually begged France and Britain for help against an encroaching Germany, they did nothing. Russia was forced to sign its own Non-Aggression Pact with Hitler. This secured Hitler's vital eastern front against invasion, allowing him to start World War II.

A Fatally Flawed Treaty

The Treaty of Versailles that settled World War I was a treaty of revenge. France wanted to insure that Germany would never again pose a threat. It pushed for a treaty that was extraordinarily one-sided and punitive. The Treaty's flaws fueled the German resentment that Hitler used to seize power. The Treaty had four fundamental failings.

First, there was no formal surrender of the German state following the armistice of 1918. Fighting simply stopped and the settlement conference began. This was quite unusual in the history of western wars. But the fact of no formal surrender would later be seized upon by Hitler to declare that the German people had not been defeated on the battlefield but, rather, had been "stabbed in the back" by traitors wanting to destroy Germany from within. The German military, humiliated by its defeat in the War, backed this story.

Second, the Treaty's War Guilt Clause (paragraph 231) made Germany and Germany alone responsible for all of the destruction resulting from the War. Germany was certainly the primary aggressor but it was hardly alone in waging four continuous years of industrialized slaughter. The admission of solitary war guilt would weigh unbearably on the German people over the next two decades. They would come to feel it was their duty to clear their honor—by starting another war.

Third, the Treaty imposed crushing reparations—requirements for repayment—upon the German people. These reparations were related to the War Guilt Clause. France, humiliated from the second invasion by Germany in less than 50 years, wanted Germany punished so badly it would never recover. The burden of reparations contributed to a breakdown of the German economy in the early 1920s. Out of the ashes of that destruction emerged the great villain of World War II, Adolph Hitler.

Finally, the partitioning of Eastern Europe virtually guaranteed future German aggression. The Treaty created eight new countries in Eastern Europe. The purposes in creating these countries were three-fold: to penalize Germany; to provide national self-determination to ethnic peoples who had been governed by empires; and to create a *Cordon Sanitaire*, or sanitary corridor, to isolate Russia from the West.

Millions of ethnic Germans were caught up in these new countries, including in Austria, Czechoslovakia, Poland, Hungary, and Yugoslavia. Repatriating these people became one of Hitler's most persistent justifications for his escalating aggression.

The cumulative effect of the Treaty was to enrage the German people who called it a "slave treaty." The Treaty also divided the Allies against themselves. The French felt it should have been even more punitive. The British felt the penalties were overdone. The hatred the Treaty evoked caused the Americans to distance themselves from it altogether. In these ways, the Treaty virtually assured hostility from Germany and a divided front by the Allies in enforcing the post-War peace.

U.S. Isolation

One of the supreme ironies of World War I was that while it thrust the U.S. into the position of the most powerful nation in the world, it also resulted in the U.S. withdrawing into itself, rejecting involvement in the affairs of Europe and turning to isolation. At any other time this might not have had such negative consequences. But with Europe so damaged as a result of the War, it left a vacuum in world leadership. The fate of the continent and the world was left to be shaped by either the weakest or the most sinister actors.

U.S. president Woodrow Wilson proposed a settlement for the War that was based on ideas of openness, justice, and self-determination. These ideas were summarized in his *Fourteen Points,* which he offered as the basis for the Versailles Treaty. But France was more interested in revenge, while Britain wanted to protect its damaged but still extensive global empire. Since the War and its settlement were mainly European affairs, the Treaty ended up being driven by these latter considerations and, thus, was deeply flawed.

The U.S. Congress never did ratify the Treaty. The entangling alliances that had started the War and the rancor and hidden agendas that surrounded the Treaty repulsed Americans, who greatly distrusted European intrigue. Nor did the U.S. ever join Wilson's proposed League of Nations, a fact that undermined the League's effectiveness. As a result of these two acts, the U.S. surrendered leadership in world affairs. It retreated behind two oceans while the affairs of Europe unraveled.

In 1922, for example, and again in the 1930s, the U.S. enacted a set of high tariffs to protect its own industries from international competition. But since the U.S. was the largest economy in the world, these tariffs made it difficult for other nations to sell to it. Without the ability to sell to the U.S. market, Germany, in particular, could not pay its reparations. And the Allies could not repay the money they had borrowed from the U.S. during the War. Worse, U.S. tariffs triggered retaliatory tariffs from other nations and a downward economic spiral in the entire global economy. It was during this Great Depression that Adolph Hitler came to power.

Also in the 1930s, the U.S. passed the *Neutrality Acts.* Their intent was to keep the U.S. from becoming enmeshed in foreign wars. U.S. policy would favor neither the aggressor nor the victim country. But their effect was perverse. When Italy invaded Ethiopia in 1935, the Acts effectively favored Italy by allowing coal, oil and other supplies to continue flowing. In the Spanish Civil War, the Acts effectively favored the fascists—the aggressors—fighting to overthrow the popularly elected republican government.

In other words, by purporting to remain neutral economically, American policy implicitly favored the aggressor. And by trying to stay out of political affairs, the U.S. failed to shore up the weakened democratic states of Europe against fascist aggression. In the lead-up to Munich, President Roosevelt declared, "The government of the United States will assume no obligations in the conduct of the present negotiations." Similarly, at the height of the second Czechoslovakian crisis, Roosevelt stated, "It would be 100% wrong to believe that the United States is going to get involved to solve what is, in truth, a European problem." Of course, the U.S. did eventually become involved, but only after it was dragged into the greatest war the world has ever known.

4 The Slowly Unfolding Crisis

Though the European state system had been badly damaged by the War, it was not yet in crisis. That would take another decade and would unfold slowly. It began with a perilously unstable government in Germany that unleashed one of the most destructive inflations of modern times. It gained steam with the creation of fascism in Italy and its later adoption in Germany and Japan. The Great Depression destroyed normal politics in Europe and helped unleash the forerunner to World War II, the Spanish Civil War. And most importantly, the period saw the rise of Adolph Hitler.

The Weimar Republic

The Weimar Republic was created in the aftermath of the collapse of Germany in World War I. It was named for the city, Weimar, in which the constitution was written. The new constitution prescribed a classic liberal parliamentary democracy. But Germany had had virtually no experience with democracy. It had been an authoritarian constitutional monarchy in the run up to the War. So it was beset by problems almost from the very beginning.

First, the forces that had begun, fought, and lost the War—the monarchy, the military, the industrialists, the financiers, and the major agricultural interests— would not accept responsibility for defeat. They believed that if they adopted the guise of liberal democratic institutions Germany would receive more lenient treatment at Versailles. When this proved a false hope, they set about to destroy the liberal government itself. Their reasons were straightforward.

Success of the left would advertise the failure of the right. Moreover, success by the left would legitimize republican government, so hated by the right. So the rightists did everything they could to undermine the elected government. They used parliamentary maneuver, shifting coalitions, domination of the new mass media, legislative obstruction, staged public relations spectacles, relentless pressure by narrow but powerful interests, judicial intimidation and, eventually, outright murder of their political opponents. Eventually they succeeded.

The Great Inflation of the early Twenties did much to delegitimize the Weimar government. It was from the collapse that followed the inflation that Hitler first gained notoriety. And the parliamentary structure of the government, with eight major parties and many more minor ones, made it all but impossible to hold together a stable majority. It also made it easy to block essential legislation. It was almost a prescription for failure.

Finally, it was the liberals who had signed the hated Treaty of Versailles on behalf of the German government, a fact the rightists advertised at every turn. When the economy crashed in the Great Depression, it was easy to blame everything on the Weimar government. Hitler did so and convinced President Paul von Hindenburg (the general who had lost the War) to name him Chancellor.

German Inflation

In 1914, the German government began printing money to pay for the expenses of the War. It was an easy thing for the government to do since it controlled the printing press. It simply printed more money to buy whatever it needed. By the end of the War, it had "inflated" the money supply by 400% with the consequence that everything cost more than triple what it did before the War.

After the War, the government was faced with both a damaged economy and the burden of paying reparations to the Allies. The temptation to print money proved irresistible. But with more money chasing the same number of goods, prices rose ever faster in what became known as an "inflationary spiral." By the beginning of 1922, the government had increased the money supply by another 1000%. A pair of shoes that had cost 1 mark in 1914 cost 80 marks just seven years later—80 *times* as much. In the next twelve months, the process accelerated as the government printed more and more and still more money.

By the end of 1922, the 1 mark pair of shoes cost 42,000 marks. Money was becoming worthless. The government was employing 30 paper mills and 2000 printing presses, all running around the clock issuing ever more worthless money. The printers felt it a waste to put ink onto paper that made it worth so much less than the ink itself. By November 1923, the government had inflated the money supply by four *trillion* times. When the scheme finally exploded, the 1 mark pair of shoes had risen in price to 75,000,000 marks. There was no reliable standard of value. The German economy collapsed.

The German middle class was destroyed. Many Germans had held jobs or pensions whose payments were fixed by contract. At one time, one hundred marks per month provided for a comfortable living or retirement. But by the time the inflation was over, it wouldn't buy a toothpick. Millions of honest, hard working Germans were bankrupted. One of the only groups to escape devastation was the Jews. Jews had historically kept their wealth in gold. The value of gold rose with inflation, leaving Jewish fortunes intact while millions of others were destroyed.

Looking for answers to what had happened, more and more Germans turned to the angry scapegoating of Adolph Hitler. Hitler declared that the collapse of the economy wasn't the Germans' fault. Rather, they had been "stabbed in the back" by the punitive reparations of the Versailles Treaty and "traitorous Jews." It was a deceitful, if appealing, message for it absolved the German people of responsibility for their own situation. The Nobel Prize-winning German novelist, Thomas Mann, stated in 1942, "A straight line runs from the madness of the German inflation to the madness of the Third Reich."

The Rise of Fascism

Fascism was a new form of government developed by Benito Mussolini, leader of Italy, in the early 1920s. It was neither communist, like Russia's government, nor democratic, like Britain's. Rather, it was a capitalist dictatorship. A form of fascism—Nazi-ism—was adopted by Germany under Hitler. Japan implemented a still different variant under Emperor Hirohito in the 1930s. Fascism has four distinguishing characteristics.

The first characteristic of fascism is a close alliance between government and big business. Hitler used the fear of communism to secure the support of big business interests for his rise to power. In return, Hitler directed state spending through these businesses while outlawing labor unions. He also used the power of the state to enslave millions of workers who were forced to labor in the mines and factories of his big business allies.

The second characteristic of fascism is nationalist aggression. All three of the fascist governments between the Wars used nationalist aggression to acquire new territory and to whip their peoples into nationalistic fervor supporting the state. Manchuria, Austria, Czechoslovakia, Ethiopia, China, and Albania were all invaded under the banner of fascist-driven nationalist aggression.

The third characteristic of fascism is single-party rule. In none of the fascist countries were competing parties tolerated. In Italy, the fascists deployed "blackshirts"—bands of thugs—to intimidate and in some cases murder opposition figures. In Japan, militarist fervor allowed only loyalty to the Emperor. Germany adopted the model of Italy, employing "brownshirts" to harass, threaten, and sometimes kill members of the opposition. When Hitler assumed power in 1933 as the head of the National Socialist party, he quickly outlawed all competing parties.

The fourth characteristic of fascism is the suppression of civil liberties. Fascism declares that the state is the supreme political entity. All political expression must be mediated by the state. All loyalty is due the state. As a consequence, all individual rights must be subordinated to the state. When Hitler became Chancellor in 1933, he immediately outlawed political dissent. His S.A. and S.S. police organizations ruthlessly intimidated opposition. Freedom of speech, press, and assembly were all taken away.

In 1937, Italy, Germany, and Japan signed the Rome-Berlin-Tokyo Pact, promising to work together to further fascist aims, including resisting the spread of communism. These became the "Axis Powers" fighting the Allies in World War II.

Japanese Aggression in Asia

While Germany and Italy were rising to power in Europe, Japan had already begun its territorial expansion in Asia. It had occupied Korea in 1898 and set its ambitions to acquiring a European-style empire. It had startled the world by defeating Russia in the Russo-Japanese War of 1905. And as a payback for its support of the Allies in World War I, Japan was given some of the German colonies in Asia. But Japan's ambitions for empire eventually collided with U.S. expansion in the Pacific. This collision would bring the two nations to war.

In 1931, Japan invaded and took over the northern Chinese province of Manchuria. This act is considered by many historians to be the first major territorial aggression leading to World War II. The League of Nations condemned the action, but Japan quit the League in 1933 and nothing was done. The truth was that the European-dominated League saw the problems of Asia as far removed from its own. And Japan proved useful in keeping Russian forces occupied outside of Europe. Finally, the U.S. was unwilling to forgo its profitable trade with Japan and refused to go along with economic sanctions.

Japan continued its attacks in China's northern provinces throughout 1934 and 1935. In 1937,

Japan attacked China proper. Its assault on the city of Nanking, known as The Rape of Nanking, killed an estimated 300,000 people. It is still recognized as one of the most heinous attacks on civilians of all time. By this time, however, Europe was even more embroiled in its own problems and no country was willing to confront the Japanese. Britain, which had the greatest capacity to deter Japanese aggression, also had extensive commercial interests in east Asia and did nothing.

Japan's imperial ambition could only be realized if it had access to industrial raw materials—oil, coal, iron, rubber, tin, etc.—but it had few of these on its own small islands. In September 1940, it attacked French Indochina (today's Vietnam, Laos, and Cambodia). In response, the U.S. placed a naval embargo on oil and other strategic materials going to Japan. Such an embargo meant certain economic strangulation. The U.S. also froze all Japanese assets in the United States and demanded Japan remove its troops from China and French Indochina.

These terms would have meant the end of Japanese imperial ambitions in Asia. The Japanese also believed that it would mean eventual colonization of Japan by the white race, the way the rest of Asia had been colonized. Japan refused the U.S.'s demands and instead, on December 7, 1941, attacked the U.S. fleet at Pearl Harbor in Hawaii. Four days later, Germany declared war on the U.S. Whereas only a week before the U.S. was not a combatant at all, it was now involved in both the Pacific and European theaters of World War II.

The Great Depression

Between 1924, at the end of the Great Inflation, and 1929, the German economy enjoyed something of a revival. But beginning in late 1929, the economies of the capitalist world suffered a catastrophic breakdown. Worldwide industrial production fell by over one third. Agricultural prices declined by one half. International commerce (trade between countries) dropped by 60%. Tens of millions of people found themselves with no jobs, no resources, and no prospects. Never before in modern history had the world's economy suffered such a crushing collapse.

The Great Depression, as it came to be called, hit especially hard in Germany. The Great Inflation of the early 1920s had destroyed massive amounts of private wealth, making the economy perilously dependent on foreign loans. Germany was particularly dependent on loans from the United States. But the 1929 stock market crash in the U.S., which had triggered the Depression, made it impossible for the U.S. to continue loaning money to Germany. As a result, the German economy completely broke down.

Thousands of factories, banks, and businesses were closed. In 1930, two million German workers were unemployed. By 1933 that figure had risen to nine million, 45% of the entire German workforce.

Tens of millions of people were made bankrupt, their life savings destroyed, again. The Great War had been a first devastating blow to the German economy. The Great Inflation was a second. And the Great Depression was the final blow.

Adolph Hitler, a supreme political opportunist, seized once again on the anger, fear, and desperation of the German people. Hitler claimed that the government had failed its duty to the German people and that only he could save the country from even further devastation. In the elections of 1930, Hitler's National Socialist (Nazi) Party went from holding 12 seats in the national government to holding 107, second only to the leading Socialist party. By 1932, his Nazi party polled 37% of all votes in the national election. This paved the way to Hitler being appointed Chancellor in January 1933.

The Spanish Civil War

The Spanish Civil War provided a "dress rehearsal" of sorts for World War II. From 1936 to 1939, it pitted the forces of fascism against an established republican government. The fascists won, but it was how they won that sent such frightening signals to the rest of the world.

In 1930, Spain was ruled by an autocratic Bourbon monarch, King Alphonso XIII. The Roman Catholic church held great sway in the public and private lives of the people. The economy was retrograde, income was concentrated in very few hands, and the mass of people were desperately poor. However, elections in 1931 placed the country's first-ever representative government into power. It proceeded with a program of public education, public health, and land reform.

But the new government was immediately attacked by a coalition of ultra-conservative monarchists, the Catholic Church, and the landed aristocracy. The government survived but by 1936 was forced by its right-wing opponents to hold new elections. Again, a majority of the Spanish people voted for the republicans, thwarting the rightists' ambitions of takeover. This time, however, the opponents, who called themselves "nationalists," attacked with weapons, starting a civil war that waged for the next three years.

The right wing, led by fascist general Francisco Franco, received extensive help from fascist Italy and Germany. Italy provided some 700 aircraft, 2,000 cannons, 250,000 rifles, and 50,000 men. Germany sent tanks, aircraft, men, and munitions and used the war as a vehicle for testing the weapons and battlefield tactics it would soon use in the larger war to come. The Spanish government appealed for help to democratic governments in Britain, France, and the United States. France promised aid but sent little. Britain and the United States sent nothing. The Soviet Union sent 2,000 men and a small amount of arms and ammunition to help defend the democratically elected government from fascist takeover.

Against the vastly better armed forces of the opposition, the republican government was eventually defeated in 1939. Over 600,000 people were killed during the Spanish Civil War. Franco ruled Spain until his death in 1975. The fact that democratic governments *would* not defend democracy in Spain while fascist governments helped their allies created an ominous precedent for Europe. It helped embolden Hitler as he time and again challenged the passivity of democratic governments on the way to war.

The Rise of Adolph Hitler

Adolph Hitler was the towering figure of the InterWar Years. Without Hitler, it is unlikely that Europe would have ever returned to war. It was Hitler's vision of world conquest and his evil, manic genius that drove Germany to seek through war what it was too impatient to attempt by peaceful means. His background, his rise to power, and his extraordinary character are all important in understanding how Germany convinced itself to start World War II.

Hitler was born in Austria and became a German citizen when he was 43 years old. From the time he was 16 until he was 25, Hitler was basically a bum. He drifted around Vienna and, later, Munich working odd jobs and fancying himself an artist and philosopher. In 1914, he joined the German army to fight in World War I. He proved himself a good soldier and was twice decorated for bravery. The War ended while Hitler was still in the hospital recovering from exposure to mustard gas. The German surrender struck Hitler hard. He refused to believe the German army had been defeated.

After the War, he joined a small group of political activists to form the German Worker's Party. Hitler soon became leader of the party and renamed it the National Socialist German Worker's Party, or "Nazi" Party, for short. Hitler's ambition got ahead of him when he tried to overthrow the German government in 1923 from a beer hall in Munich. The famous "Beer Hall Putsch" landed Hitler in jail. He used the time to write *Mein Kampf,* his vision for how he would take power and lead the German people to become "lords of the earth." Once out of jail, Hitler began organizing a viable national political party. By 1928, the Nazi party had enlisted only 110,000 members.

The Great Depression proved a godsend to Hitler. His campaign promised jobs for every German and repudiation of the Treaty of Versailles. It was a compelling story. In the elections of 1930, the Nazi party received 6.5 million votes, making it the number two party in Germany. Still, this was only 19% of all votes, far from a majority needed to rule. By 1932, as the Depression worsened, Hitler's party received 13.5 million votes, or 37% of the total. It was the highest total he would ever receive under democratic auspices. Still, he was denied a role in government leadership.

In 1933, Hitler made a deal with the aristocrats, generals, and business leaders who controlled the government. If they appointed him Chancellor, he would ban labor unions, repudiate the Treaty of Versailles, and rebuild the military. On that basis, Hitler was appointed Chancellor on January 30, 1933. He kept his promises. He also banned all competing political parties, and suspended civil liberties. In what became known as The Night of the Long Knives, Hitler purged the government of opposition, murdering more than 1,000 opponents, including many from his own Nazi party. Hitler had risen to power by legal means but then used unconstitutional means to consolidate that power, making himself dictator of Germany.

Hitler's character was startling. He was an intensely angry and hateful person. Yet he possessed an unquestioned genius for politics, both national and international. He was the most brilliant orator of his day, holding crowds of hundreds of thousands mesmerized for hours at a time. He had enormous willpower and used it to intimidate those who opposed him. He was a ruthless liar and a supreme opportunist with an incomparable sense for when to act and when to wait. Most of all, Hitler had a deep sense of the longing of the German people for respect and glory and a knowledge of how to play to it. These traits made him master of Germany and destroyer of Europe.

5   The Path to War

From the end of World War I in 1918 until Hitler's coming to power in 1933, Germany made a concerted effort to right itself from the destruction of the First World War. It established the Weimar Republic, the first representative government in German history. It worked (not always to the best effect) to restore the economic vigor that had long been such an essential part of its character. And it did the best it could to re-integrate itself into the community of nations. It did these things in the context of the international rule of law.

But with Hitler's appointment as Chancellor in 1933 and his assumption of the Presidency in 1934, German rebuilding took on a wholly different character: it became fascistic, ultra-nationalistic, and militarily expansionist. By 1939, German aggression would trigger the start of World War II. Six events are especially noteworthy as they demarcate this path to War.

Rearmament

One of the most important provisions of the Treaty of Versailles was that Germany agreed to limitations on the size of its military. In October 1933, nine months after Hitler became Chancellor, Germany quit the League of Nations and the disarmament convention that the League had sponsored. Hitler condemned the League as an effort to enforce a status quo that kept Germany "enslaved." He announced the terms on which Germany would agree to return to the League, terms that were intended to be refused.

Those terms would have allowed Germany to have an army 50% larger than that authorized by the Treaty. They would have precluded any inspections or controls over the German military by international bodies. They also stipulated that no account be made of the private SS and SA armies that Hitler commanded independent of the German state military. These terms were unacceptable to the League and its major members. But neither the League nor any of its member nations did anything, save for issuing verbal condemnations. It was a fateful—though only the first—capitulation to Hitler's aggression.

In March 1935, Hitler went still further. He announced that an air force, which was forbidden under the Treaty, in fact already existed. Germany had built it in secret, in the Soviet Union, and with the help of the Soviet government. He also announced a return to military conscription for the purpose of rebuilding the German army. As with the October

1933 announcements, these were in naked violation of the Treaty of Versailles. And as with the earlier offenses, they were condemned with words but were not confronted with action.

The fact that neither Britain nor France challenged Hitler's violation of the Treaty served to make Hitler increasingly bold in his future aggressions. Worse, in June 1935, Britain announced its own naval treaty with Germany that effectively gutted the limitations written into Versailles. Britain had begun dealing with Germany directly in order to take care of its own interests. Its actions undercut its main ally, France, and proved the last nail in the coffin of the collective security regime of Versailles. From here it would be every man (nation) for himself.

Invasion of the Rhineland

The Rhine River valley forms a natural boundary between Germany and France. The Treaty of Versailles stipulated that this area—known as the Rhineland—should be demilitarized, kept free from military forces of either side. It was believed that if armies did not face each other directly there would be less likelihood of war. In addition to its coerced agreement at Versailles, Germany had also voluntarily agreed to this demilitarization of the Rhineland in the Treaty of Locarno, which it signed with Britain, France, and Italy in 1925.

In March 1936, Germany marched 150,000 men into the Rhineland, remilitarizing the region. The move destroyed the Versailles and Locarno conditions of demilitarization. The world was shocked that Germany should so nakedly repudiate its own treaty obligations. People still believed in the diplomacy of gentlemen. But just as when Germany re-armed in 1935, the western democracies did nothing. The French, despite having the largest army in Europe, said they would not act without British backing. Britain refused to back military action. The League of Nations condemned the invasion but it, too, did nothing.

The Rhineland invasion marked a critical turning point. First, it was the first German territorial expansion outside of the boundaries laid down at Versailles—even though it was an expansion within Germany itself. Second, it greatly elevated Hitler's prestige within Germany. The invasion had been vigorously resisted by German generals who believed it risked retaliation by France. France had a much superior army and even Hitler admitted that if France had fought the invasion, "We would have had to withdraw with our tail between our legs." But Hitler had been certain that neither France nor Britain would contest his action. He was proven right. His confidence in his own judgment and his standing with his generals soared.

Finally, the Rhineland is considered one of the last times Hitler could have been stopped short of actual military hostilities. The fact that the democracies did not resist German aggression revealed their moral incapacity for action. There was no question that the occupation was blatantly illegal. Britain and France had more than enough military might to reverse Germany's move. But they could not muster the will for confrontation. From that point on, their own feebleness fed on itself, undermining their own belief in their ability to stand up to evil.

Anschluss

Although the Treaty of Versailles had made Austria an independent state, Austria was still fundamentally a Germanic nation. Hitler, a native Austrian himself, had always longed for its reunification with Germany. In 1934, Austrian Nazis, supported by their German counterparts, attempted a *coup d'etat* of the Austrian government, murdering the Chancellor, Engelbert Dollfuss. The coup failed but did not deter Nazi ambitions.

In February 1938, Hitler summoned Dollfuss' replacement, Kurt von Schuschnigg, to Germany where he ordered Schuschnigg to effectively turn over the Austrian government. Schuschnigg refused and instead announced a referendum to determine whether the Austrian people wished to remain independent. Hitler was enraged, knowing that the outcome would thwart his plans for takeover. On March 11, 1938, a Nazi minister acting on Hitler's orders announced that *he* was Chancellor of Austria. He immediately issued a request for the German military to enter Austria "to restore order." Two hundred thousand German troops marched into

Austria the next day. (This event forms the backdrop for the popular movie, "The Sound of Music.")

The Anschluss, as the reunification was called, was noteworthy for three things. First, it was the beginning of Hitler's territorial expansion outside Germany. Second, like the Rearmament and the occupation of the Rhineland before it, it was a naked violation of the terms of the Versailles Treaty. Third, and most important, despite having publicly declared that they would support Austria's independence, neither France nor Britain did anything. France was torn by political factionalism and would not act without British support. The British Prime Minister, Neville Chamberlain, actually supported Hitler's aggression, stating publicly that he understood the German desire for re-unification. Once again, acquiescence emboldened Hitler by showing him that the democracies had no stomach for confrontation.

Sudetenland/Munich

Like Austria, Czechoslovakia had been created in the settlement of World War I. Also like Austria, a significant portion of Czechoslovakia's population was German. The western part of Czechoslovakia, the Sudetenland, was more than 50% German. Hitler wanted this territory for its superb industrial assets and as a launching pad for the eventual conquest of Russia. In 1936, Czechoslovakian Nazis, goaded by Nazis in Germany, began a campaign of agitation against the Czech government. They were suppressed, but in September 1938, Hitler used the excuse of "persecution of the German people" to demand that the Sudetenland be handed over to Germany. He threatened military action if this was not done.

By this time, many European leaders had begun to understand Hitler's aggressive intentions. In May 1938, Neville Chamberlain, Prime Minister of Britain, issued a warning to Hitler against invading Czechoslovakia. But even as he issued this warning, he made public statements saying that Britain was not prepared to go to war to defend Czechoslovakia. The Russians, fearful of German aggression, asked the British for help should Hitler move to take Czechoslovakia. Chamberlain declined. The French, who actually had a formal treaty with Czechoslovakia to come to its defense if it were attacked, said they would only help if the British would. The British wouldn't. The French asked the U.S. for help. The U.S. declined.

In September 1938, at a fateful meeting in Munich, Britain, Italy, France, and Germany agreed on a plan to carve up Czechoslovakia, giving the German parts to Germany and leaving the rest to be sorted out later. Russia, which was best situated to help defend Czechoslovakia, had been intentionally excluded from the meeting. In exchange, Hitler agreed not to destroy the country. There were no Czech representatives at the meeting. On his return to London, Chamberlain made one of the most catastrophically mistaken prophesies of modern diplomacy: he declared he had delivered "peace for our time." Nothing could have been further from the truth.

Once again, Hitler had challenged the democracies for illegal acquisition of territory and won—all without firing a shot. In fact, it was the British and French governments who did Hitler's dirty work—telling the Czech leader, Edward Benes, that *their* governments insisted he give up his country in order to keep peace in central Europe. The names Munich and Chamberlain became synonymous with appeasement—trying to stop aggression by giving in to the aggressor.

As with Austria, the successful acquisition of Czechoslovakia emboldened Hitler further. As he was plotting the takeover of the rest of Czechoslovakia in the spring of 1939, Hitler assured his generals that there would be no need for military force. "Our enemies are worms," he declared. "I saw them at Munich."

The Rest of Czechoslovakia

Czechoslovakia had always been a "synthetic" nation. It was created in the settlement of World War I with three purposes in mind: to punish Germany by carving off part of its territory; to give self-determination to the millions of ethnic Czechs and Slovaks living there; and to isolate Russia and its communist "plague" from the West. Rather than being a nation of states, it was a state of nations: a conglomeration of Czechs, Slovaks, Germans, Poles, Hungarians, Ruthenians,

Slavs, and a smattering of other ethnic groups. Czechoslovakia could only survive as an independent country if guaranteed protection by the Great Powers who had created it. But those Powers—Britain and France—withdrew that guarantee by allowing Hitler to dismember Czechoslovakia at Munich. It was only a matter of time, therefore, before the rest the country disintegrated or was taken over.

The takeover occurred in March 1939. Hitler had befriended the Slovaks after Munich, encouraging them to carry out mischief against the government as the Sudeten Germans had the year before. When the government moved to suppress their disorder, Hitler, following the familiar pattern of Austria and Munich, moved in to "restore order." On March 15, 1939, the president of the Slovak Republic (what was left of Czechoslovakia after Munich), Emil Hacha, signed an agreement making it a protectorate of Germany. German troops occupied the country immediately. Czechoslovakia ceased to exist.

The Western signatories to the Munich settlement, Britain, France, and Italy, had guaranteed the integrity of the remaining Slovakian Republic. But again, as they had already done three times before, they did nothing. Hitler had further advanced his expansionary objectives without firing a shot. Neville Chamberlain, the British architect of appeasement, declared that there was no use in Britain mounting a defense of a country that had ceased to exist. It was an astoundingly cynical attempt to exonerate himself and his country from an obligation he had always preferred to not have to honor.

By now, however, there could be no remaining credibility for the policy of appeasement. Making repeated concessions to Hitler's demands clearly did not stop him from raising ever more of them. Rather, it simply made him bolder and more self-confident in devising ever greater demands. His next exploit, the one that would trigger World War II, was aimed at Poland.

Berlin-Moscow Non-Aggression Pact/Poland

By now Hitler had rearmed, taken the Rhineland, unified Germany with Austria, annexed the Sudetenland, and seized the rest of Czechoslovakia. It was clear that he intended to swallow at least all of Eastern Europe and possibly Western Europe and the Soviet Union as well. In the spring of 1939 the Soviet Union approached Britain to try to arrange for mutual defense against Germany's relentless advance.

But while Britain was happy to have Soviet help against a German attack on Britain, Chamberlain would not commit Britain to a reciprocal obligation—helping the Soviet Union should it be attacked by Germany. The Soviets were certain that Germany intended to attack Poland, which lay between them, and, then, the Soviet Union itself. That plan had been laid out in *Mein Kampf,* in which Hitler clearly stated that his goal was the conquest of the Slavic race and its territories. Unable to secure Western help to fend off a German attack, Stalin signed a Non-Aggression Pact with Germany in August 1939.

The pact defined which parts of Poland each country would get, should either of them invade. It was like a big wink. With no threat of retaliation from the Soviet Union to his east, Hitler invaded Poland only a week later, on September 1, 1939. Two days later, Britain and France each declared war on Germany, marking the beginning of World War II. The Soviet Union invaded Poland two weeks later, on September 17, 1939. By the end of September, Poland ceased to exist.

As with so much of its InterWar diplomacy, Britain's handling of the Soviet Union was a massive blunder. Despite their common interests in deterring German aggression, the British could never see past their hatred of communism. In August 1939, before the Berlin-Moscow Non-Aggression Pact was signed, Chamberlain was asked whether Russia might not be a useful ally against Germany. Chamberlain replied, "I have very deep suspicions about that country." Just before the negotiations at Munich he has said of Hitler, "I have the greatest respect for this man." Chamberlain preferred what he thought were the certainties of a dictatorial fascist capitalism to the uncertainties of an expedient alliance with communists. His miscalculation drove his two worst enemies—Germany and Russia—together. It also started World War II.

6 Reflections

It is the enigmas of the InterWar years that so puzzle the historical imagination. Two of the greatest of these are why the Germans so embraced Hitler, and why the Western democracies were unable to stop him.

Why the Germans Embraced Hitler

At the beginning of the twentieth century, Germany was one of the most sophisticated societies in the world. Over the centuries, it had produced such geniuses as Gutenberg, Luther, Mozart, Kant, Beethoven, Einstein, and Freud. It had developed by far the most powerful economy in Europe. Its people were wealthy, literate, inventive, industrious, and cosmopolitan. How is it, then, that these same people embraced—indeed idolized—Hitler, one of the crudest, most thuggish leaders of all time?

First, Hitler always gave the German people someone else to blame for their problems. The Germans never wanted to believe that they had actually lost World War I. Hitler told them they hadn't: they had been "stabbed in the back" by traitorous liberals. They didn't want to believe that the ruinous inflation of 1923 was their own fault. Hitler told them it wasn't: it was the work of "Jew financiers." They didn't want to believe the economic collapse of the Depression was their fault (it wasn't entirely). Hitler blamed the communists.

Second, Hitler made the German people feel important. He told them that they were superior to other people, that they were a "master race." He told them that it was their destiny to rule Europe and, eventually, the world. He told them that they would be the foundation of a "Thousand Year Reich" that would spread the blessings of German culture to the rest of the world. Perhaps it is true that people who are beaten down—as the German people undoubtedly were—are uniquely susceptible to such flattery. Hitler made them feel big and part of something even bigger and they worshiped him for it.

Finally, Hitler made the German people's lives very comfortable—at least until the ending years of World War II. Never once did he raise taxes on German working people. Everybody had jobs. He introduced social benefits that were among the most generous in the world. Massive public works programs built highways and civic structures throughout the country. He paid German soldiers twice what soldiers in other countries received. In all of these ways, the material quality of German life was exceptional. Of course, this could be done only by conquering other countries, enslaving other people, and plundering their wealth. And it required the imposition of a police state, the elimination of civil liberties, and the suppression of all political opposition within Germany. But it was a bargain the German people willingly, readily embraced.

There was, in other words, a profound illusoriness behind the German people's embrace of Hitler: a readiness to blame others for their own problems; a need to be dishonestly flattered; a deceitful willingness to receive something for nothing. The collapse of the Weimar Republic in 1933 showed the German people's political immaturity as well: their unwillingness to govern themselves. This desire to live in a fantasy world is what allowed the German people to pretend they knew nothing of the monstrous genocide of six million Jews that had been advertised for years and that was carried out with their complicity, under their own noses, during World War II. Before this blissful ignorance had run its course, it would cause the deaths of more than 50 million human beings.

Why the Western Democracies Couldn't Stop Hitler
A second lurking question haunts the InterWar years: Why were the Western democracies unable to stop Hitler? Until Poland in 1939, most of Hitler's aggressions could have been stopped by resolute resistance from the democratic powers. Hitler himself admitted this. The fact that his bluffs always worked

was a source of wonder to his military advisers. Hitler used each instance of Western capitulation to build his self-confidence and his reputation for political genius. But what was it about the character of the democracies—really Britain and France—that made them incapable of standing up to such naked aggression? Three answers come to mind.

First, the Western democracies were simply terrified of another war. This was an artifact of the horror of World War I. As much as the 26 million casualties, it was the combatants' inability to stop the carnage that had so traumatized the participants. If another World War started, would they be able to stop themselves this time? The leaders of Britain and France were so afraid of the unforeseeable consequences of another war, they did everything possible to avoid conflict. Unfortunately, they failed to recognize that caving in to aggression does not deter it: it only makes it bolder. Each time they gave in to Hitler's threats, they made him even more confident that still greater concessions could be gained by threatening again. And he was right. Until the very end, every one of Hitler's gains was achieved without a single shot being fired.

Second, World War I had profoundly damaged the democracies' belief in themselves. They had fancied themselves the most civilized of cultures, superior to all other people on earth. They had built an international political system based on rationality, diplomacy, and a balance of powers. But that system had failed to prevent the greatest man-made catastrophe in the history of the world. And the collapse had happened so quickly they hadn't had time to devise a new system. Hence, Versailles. The economic foundations of the capitalist world had crumbled as well. The Great Depression was an almost mortal blow to the upbeat confidence of western economic superiority. As with the collapse of political institutions, the collapse of economic institutions greatly undercut the democracies' confidence in their own systems. Simply put, Western capitalist democracies did not believe in themselves enough to stand up to evil.

A final explanation has to do with appeasement. Here, there are three alternative explanations, or theories, each worth considering. The mainstream explanation was articulated even before World War II was over. It was that British Prime Minister Neville Chamberlain was a naïve bumbler: arrogant; ignorant of the evil agenda of Hitler; overly impressed with his own logic; and perhaps cowardly. He sincerely believed Hitler could be propitiated—appeased—by giving in to his escalating demands. A more sinister version of this theory acknowledges that Chamberlain consistently misled the British public about his diplomacy and even shut out important members of his own cabinet. But the failing was still largely Chamberlain's and his alone. The larger British political culture is exonerated from any wrong-doing. Winston Churchill, who succeeded Chamberlain as

Prime Minister and helped lead the Allies to victory in World War II, contributed significantly to this interpretation.

By the 1970s, a critique of the traditional theory of appeasement had emerged in academic circles. Known as the "revisionist" theory, it held that appeasement—making concessions to the aggressor in the expectation that they would prevent war—was actually a realistic strategy to deal with the fact of national and imperial decline. In this theory, Britain's heyday was behind it and it needed to make difficult decisions to adjust the extent of its commitments to the reality of its means. The way it did this was to effectively cede Central Europe to Hitler in exchange for his leaving the British empire alone. This "deal" (you can have Central Europe but stay out of our Empire) was, in fact, an explicit point of discussion between senior British and German officials prior to Munich. In this way, the British could keep their soldiers in the colonies (which they did), keep their empire alive (which they did), and deal with Hitler and Europe later. In this reading, appeasement is not shameful and cowardly as it is in the traditional reading, but hard-nosed and realistic. And it locates responsibility not in a single, bumbling individual but in the larger apparatus of British diplomacy and policy making itself.

A final theory that has emerged since the 1990s claims that when faced with two great evils, fascism and communism, the British *chose* fascism. For all of its odious features, fascism was still based on capitalism. It still respected private property. Communism did away with private property in favor of collective ownership. The British elite, led first by Prime Minster Stanley Baldwin, and then by Chamberlain, imagined that if they allowed (or helped) fascist Germany to become strong enough, it would destroy the communist menace in Russia, much as the Germans had destroyed the tsarist regime during World War I. The month before Munich, Chamberlain wrote to the British king, stating, "Herr Hitler has made up his mind to attack Czecho-Slovakia and then proceed east." By this reading, the British were not trying to avoid a war. They were in fact trying to foster one—between Germany and the Soviet Union. Munich and all of the other capitulations were but means to help Hitler to build up and "proceed east." But never in their worst nightmares did Western leaders imagine Germany might actually ally with Russia, leaving it free to come after them instead. If this third theory is true, it proved a fateful—and almost fatal—mistake.

7 Final Word

The European system that had been crafted by Metternich at the end of the Napoleonic Wars had been destroyed in World War I. But the Europeans had not understood that. They continued as if Europe was still the center of the world. It was certainly the center of *their* world but the foundations of that world were profoundly damaged. Its political systems no longer worked as they had before. Its economic systems were breaking down. Its imperial system with colonies around the world was tottering. Its cultural systems were shaken to their foundations. And its claim to moral authority was completely destroyed.

For all of these reasons, Europe was not able to resist the rise of a malevolent dictatorship whose objective was to subordinate Europe and make it a stepping stone to world domination. Its Western leaders, wittingly or unwittingly, went along with and even abetted Hitler's escalating aggression while repeatedly rejecting Soviet appeals to form a united front against him. They had chosen to ride the back of a tiger, surrendering control of when—and how—they could get off.

The ironic fact of this period is that the two countries that would come to assume the mantle of power after the Second World War, the United States and the Soviet Union, were almost completely absent from Europe during this period, except, that is, for the ghost of communism that haunted Europe. Europe's unwillingness to engage these two countries to help it manage its recovery after the First World War made it impossible to provide for its own security or stability. It would leave Europe at the mercy of these two superpowers after the next War. Europe would become their playground, but Europe would not again be the leading global player it once was.

8 Timeline

1918   End of WWI
        Weimar Republic formed

1919   Treaty of Versailles signed

1922   Mussolini establishes fascist government
        in Italy

        France occupies Ruhr region to try to
        collect reparations

        Rapallo Treaty between Germany
        and Soviet Union spooks Western
        democracies

1923   Great Inflation wipes out German
        middle class

        Beer Hall Putsch: Hitler jailed for
        attempted coup against Weimar
        government

1924   Dawes Plan restructures reparations
        payments, making U.S. effective guarantor

Hitler released from prison; begins
building national political party

1925   Hitler publishes *Mein Kampf,* laying out
plans for world domination

Germany signs Locarno Treaty, voluntarily accepting mutual security for
Europe

1928   Kellogg-Briand Pact outlawing war as an
instrument of national policy

1929   Young Plan supersedes Dawes Plan;
resets, extends reparation payments

Stock market collapse in U.S.; beginning
of Great Depression

1930   National Socialist (Nazi) party wins 107
seats in national election

1931   Japanese invasion of Manchuria

1933   January. Hitler appointed Chancellor;
bans trade unions

February. Reichstag Fire; Hitler blames
communists

March. National emergency declared;
civil rights suspended

October. Germany quits the League of
Nations

1934	Hitler becomes President; political opposition outlawed
	Night of the Long Knives; Hitler has political opponents murdered
	Austrian Chancellor Englebert Dolfuss is murdered by Nazis
1935	Military Re-Armament; first direct violation of Versailles Treaty
	Italy invades Ethiopia; France and Britain appease
1936	Remilitarization of the Rhineland; another violation of Versailles Treaty
	Beginning of Spanish Civil War
1937	Rome-Berlin-Tokyo Axis of Fascist countries
	Chamberlain becomes Prime Minister of Britain
	Japan invades China
1938	March. Anschluss; German takeover of Austria; prohibited by Versailles
	September. Munich conference; German takeover of Sudetenland; height of appeasement by Western powers

1939	March. German annexation of rest of Czechoslovakia
	August. Berlin-Moscow Non-Aggression Pact
	September 1. German invasion of Poland; Start of World War II
1941	December. Japanese attack on Pearl Harbor starts War in Pacific
	Germany declares war on U.S.; U.S. reciprocate
	The world is at War

If you enjoyed this book, please look for all of the titles in *The Best One-Hour History* series.

- Ancient Greece
- Rome
- The Middle Ages
- The Renaissance
- The Protestant Reformation
- European Wars of Religion
- The English Civil Wars
- The Scientific Revolution
- The Enlightenment
- The American Revolution
- The French Revolution
- The Industrial Revolution
- Europe in the 1800s
- The American Civil War
- European Imperialism
- World War I
- The Interwar Years
- World War II
- The Cold War
- The Vietnam War

To learn more about each title and its expected publication date, visit: *http://onehourhistory.com*

If you could change the world for a dollar, would you?

Well, you CAN. *Now*, WILL you?

one dollar for life

One Dollar For Life™ helps American students build schools in the developing world, for a dollar. *We can help you build one, too!*

Since 2007, we've built 15 schools and 23 infrastructure projects in countries like Nepal, Haiti, Nicaragua, Kenya, Malawi, and South Africa.

Imagine if you and all of your school's students felt the pride of building a school so another child could go to school. Well, you can! For a dollar.

ODFL will help your club or school organize a fundraiser where *every dollar donated goes into a developing world project*.

Make all of your school's students into heroes! It's easy, it's fun, and it's changing the world.

All profits from
The Best One Hour History™
series go to support ODFL.

Haiti

Nepal

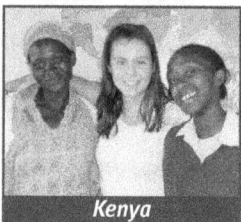
Kenya

You see, you *can* change the world. *Now*, WILL you?

Visit: odfl.org

OneDollar ForLife

email: info@odfl.org **Phone:** 661-203-8750

www.ingramcontent.com/pod-product-compliance
Lightning Source LLC
Chambersburg PA
CBHW060720030426
42337CB00017B/2937